Summer Requiem

Vikram Seth has written six books of poetry, an opera libretto and a book of other libretti. He is perhaps best known for his acclaimed novel, *A Suitable Boy*, one of the most beloved and widely read books of recent times, as well as his novels *The Golden Gate* and *An Equal Music*. He is the author of two highly regarded works of non-fiction, *From Heaven Lake* and *Two Lives*, and is currently working on *A Suitable Girl*.

Summer Requiem
a book of poems

Vikram Seth

WEIDENFELD & NICOLSON

A W&N PAPERBACK

First published in Great Britain in 2015
by Weidenfeld & Nicolson
This paperback edition published in 2016
by Weidenfeld & Nicolson
An imprint of the Orion Publishing Group Ltd
Carmelite House, 50 Victoria Embankment
London EC4Y 0DZ

An Hachette UK Company

ISBN 978 1 7802 2867 9

A CIP catalogue record for this book is available from the British Library.

Typeset in Dante by Input Data Services Ltd, Bridgwater, Somerset

Printed and bound in Great Britain by Clays Ltd, St Ives plc

The Orion Publishing Group's policy is to use papers
that are natural, renewable and recyclable products and
made from wood grown in sustainable forests. The logging
and manufacturing processes are expected to conform to
the environmental regulations of the country of origin.

www.orionbooks.co.uk

Contents

Summer Requiem

Since there is nothing left but this,
I shall watch the snakes as they twist across the plain.
They are independent of me like everything else.
Everyone I seek has a terror of intensity.
The liberated generation lives a restrained youth.
Stone by stone has been built across the mountain,
Yet people have broken their backs quietly gardening.
And whether the sheep escape or the radishes are
    blighted
Is all the same to me; I must forsake attachment.

The bells are ringing the tale of this city,
Gather and scatter, gather and scatter;
Down South, one sees the landscape flash green and
    white
'Showing no respect for space whatsoever';
In the nearby road, one shakes hands grimly.
Another is in 'a cocoon-like state' with anxiety,
Has eaten all my apricots, smiling, and now
I use my teeth as a nutcracker –
Only the stones are left, the nuts inside bitter.   ~*

* a stanza break at the end of a page is marked by ~
  no stanza break at the end of a page is marked by ⌐

Broken glass spangles the lawn;
Yesterday was revelry, so today we may not walk
    barefoot;
The shell of forgetfulness has broken sharply,
The harmony warped in my hands.
Jaggedness and discontinuity, as if the pebbles
Smoothed by centuries were crushed again.
It is clear why men wish to live where linnets call
Or the green swell is in the havens dumb.
Birds are not desolate, impute how you may.

This garden was built for peace. But every day
Somewhere a lawnmower is grumbling busily,
Building chance events into a philosophy,
'Gather and scatter, gather and scatter'.
I have so carefully mapped the corners of my mind
That I am forever waking in a lost country.
Everything learnt has been trivial: on the evening road
I fumble to read the signpost with my fingers
Which claw so fiercely they're no use at all.

Returning to the wastes of expression,
I feel again dry ground, though sterile:
From the shining sea I was thrown back always
Into the harbours of regret.
I regretted my fingernails, my eyes . . .
The town bound knots, then tore the fibres open;
The ink ran out before there were things to say.
When the sky fell upon me in a blue shudder
I was left staring at the horizon.   ~

Facts float like leaves
In my mind's calm river:
To have substance means to rot.
Cornflower and crocus have withered,
Acroclinium survives; it was always dry.
The cool of the evening brings relief to the sick fever –
Those loved eyes dead to me, those sighs stilled;
Late, late – even the rooks have flown home;
The hour of rust brings everything to a close.

Where the lock of longing was opened
There there will be a perpetual wound.
The steel cries out in grief, and there is no assuager;
Those who could have warmed are scattered,
And no one now can see the light in my window.
I stretch out my arms to the disbanded
But the flesh has pined away.
The crimson sun suspended on the dark spire
Can see me wander near the bridge.

Over the fields the pollen like last year,
The whistle of the train like – but, last year,
Last year I did not hear the whistle cry;
The sounds were a backdrop. Now with dead actors,
The canvas is all that remains of the history.
Bound and torn on the returning wheels, like pollen
Gathered and scattered, gathered and scattered,
What further pain can the future promise
To a wandering exile from heart to heart?   ~

Memory is a poison; it has sickened my body.
The cleavage of attachment has frayed my mind.
Rabid and weary, autistic, spasmodic,
Exhaustion makes me dance like a puppet.
New gargoyles are carved, new stones cleaned;
Within ten weeks the old constructs are broken;
Magnolia and tulip rushed in and out of bloom;
Rose and wistaria rush in and out of bloom;
Perpetual replacement is the only song of the world.

All striving lapsed, the reclaiming grass has covered
The brick and stone and earth and the steepest agony –
Invulnerable, cold, immune to pain;
The day sees me dreaming of sensitive hands
And of the dance of warmth across my skin.
The sun bursts through his disguise and sprinkles
Gold on the world; and the hours pass
In silent emblems of despair. Bee-filled hibiscus-filled
Summer songs underline winter.

The common air envelops the old beech.
Swinging from pain, the heart
Revels in its surroundings, and forgets; but they
Stun the air and blur my world, being absent.
In the summer's trap, one theme alone
Like the thin persistence of the flute
Upon the stifling air, attacks, attacks.
It sings that to be alive is a delicacy,
Clear filigreed glass in a vaulted hall.   ~

The evening sun retreats along the lawn;
The broken diamonds shine on the lawn;
I stand by the city wall and hear the chimes
Collect and shower sound upon the city.
The words were here, engraved in earth and weed,
The words I read too late. I can remember
I stood two years ago, where now I watch
The summer turn to bitterness and fruit
And slow unsheltering of skeletal trees.

Between the chorus of the stars and of the birds
It released itself slowly, it turned away,
And next day under the misty wave
Of need it was unwetted. Thus atrophied
The love for lack of loving, the lovers through fear.
Now only the empty doors mark empty houses;
The rusted tracks lead to dead embankments,
The signals are always down, and whistles
Are forever smearing the air with grief.

The town is indifferent; a scrapyard claw,
It lifts and deposits elsewhere on the earth's grid.
The opened rose closes, and welcomes night,
And lets the seat of joy become a grave.
Mist lifts the cold plantations of the dew.
I recreate a hunger for the dead eyes
That tuned these discordant wires and made them sing,
Walking tranquillised in the mist, under
The serene and tender evening star.   ~

Still day's death, across the fields
All swallows have flown.
The summer red sinks into the flowing dark.
From the field's corner fade the voices of the children.
Dark, as in some peace,
Twists the key of silence.
The beech proclaims power over the grasses.
Sombre thoughts become this hour,
Hour of red copper, rust, dark iron.

A Cryptic Reply

Abstractions have their place, the concrete too.
Opacity is nothing rare in you.
Prudence and love – that true link makes me smile.
A sea change may take long, or just a while.
The sun stays where it is, so does the sea.
It is the clouds and haze, the you, the me
(It's good that you imagine my concern)
That vary with the hours, burn off, or burn.

If friends are always elsewhere, never here,
Do more than just their features grow unclear?
I too will hope to look you up some day.
We each need love in our own time and way.
To ponder wholeness or to shape debris
Requires some sense of incoherency.
Since, with the tears, you sense a touch of peace,
Why hope that this or that or both should cease?

As for myself, the hope I had is gone,
And not much left in lieu to build upon.
Tale of two cities, three to be exact:
High on elation, short – I guess – on fact.
Great expectations – cue to shake my head –
Still, nothing I could wish I had not read.
My work continues, as it did before;
And sometimes I'm surprised I ask for more.

Late Light

At three the late light glides across
The last gold leaves on the black ground.
The snow is near, as is my loss:
The peaceful love I've never found.

Outside the great world's gifts and harms
There must be somewhere I can go
To rest within a lover's arms,
At ease with the impending snow.

Fellows' Garden

Despite the blights and doubts of love,
The windswept copper beech above,
Incognizant of what and why,
Tattered the puzzle of the sky.

When, snivelling on my grieving knees,
I'd feed the College tortoise peas,
The torpid glutton, on the whole,
Poured balm on my afflicted soul.

And from my unrequited heart
All Angst and Weltschmerz would depart
As spiteful mallets clicked away
A Christ Church twilight of croquet.

O mighty loves and griefs long gone,
Why won't your details linger on?
Why should it be that I recall
Beech, beast and mallet – and that's all?

Evening Across the Sky

Evening across the sky –
The glow dies in the west.
The last crows fly,
Cawing, each to its nest.
An early moon is here.
The stars appear.
Safe from all thought, all fear,
Now, heart, find rest.

Sleep dreamlessly.
Forget what chafed or held you fast.
Settle such quarrels with eternity;
The stars won't last.
The moon will die,
Earth, evening, you and I.
There are no fixtures in the sky
Free from the growing past.

Far from the City Tonight

Far from the city tonight, how bright are the stars –
How red is Betelgeuse, how red is Mars.
That such grand worlds should be mere points of light
Seen from our own seems less than strange tonight
When those worlds grand in their complexity
Known by their lesser names of you and me,
For all their flair and depth and hankerings
Hold less dimension in the scheme of things.

Can't

I find I simply can't get out of bed.
I shiver and procrastinate and stare.
I'll press the reset button in my head.

I hate my work but I am in the red.
I'd quit it all if I could live on air.
I find I simply can't get out of bed.

My joints have rusted and my brain is lead.
I drank too much last night, but now I swear
I'll press the reset button in my head.

My love has gone. What do I have instead? –
Hot-water bottle, God and teddy bear.
I find I simply can't get out of bed.

The dreams I dreamt have filled my soul with dread.
The world is mad, there's darkness everywhere.
I'll press the reset button in my head.

Who'll kiss my tears away or earn my bread?
Who'll reach the clothes hung on that distant chair?
I must, I simply must get out of bed
And press that reset button in my head.

What's in it?

I heard your name the other day
Mentioned by someone in a casual way.
She said she thought that you were looking great.
A waiter passed by with a plate.
She reached out for a sandwich, and your name
Went back from where it came.

But like a serious owlet I stood there,
Staring in mid-air.
I frowned, then followed her around
To hear, just once more, that sirenic sound –
Those consonants, those vowels – what a fool!
I show more circumspection as a rule.

I love you more than I can say.
Try as I do, it hasn't gone away.
I hoped it would once, and I hope so still.
Someday, I'm sure, it will.
No glimpse, no news, no name will stir me then.
But when? But when?

Caged

I lie awake at night, too tired to sleep,
Too fearful you should wake, too sad to weep.

I hear you breathe. I do not touch your face.
How do we live like this, caged in one space?

We two have lost each other, you and I.
Why could this not wait till our love could die?

Poor, pointless relic bent on staggering on
When courtesy and passion both have gone,

And all our energy, enhanced when paired,
And happiness, once multiplied when shared.

Light seeps out from the blind; what will it bring,
This day that could but will not change a thing? –

The litanies that bleed the heart before
It understands that it can bleed no more,

The bitter tone that taints our every speech,
The thoughts that we attribute each to each

As if we were not friends but manacled foes,
As if one sorrow were two private woes.   ~

What grew with time took time to disappear,
But now we see that there is little here.

We are ourselves; how much can we amend
Of our hard beings to appease a friend?

We cannot lose our ways, and cannot choose
To lose what then it would be peace to lose.

May love be ground away like all the rest
From those who are already dispossessed.

This Room

I love this room; this room means you to me.
The sun shines in, and sometimes music plays.
These books, this bed, this fan, that rug, these rays –
Predate and will outlast this ecstasy.
Wise to my heart, I'd rather not be free.
Let me meander on from heat to haze.
These things are everything, as are these days.
My aim will be the aim of things: to be.

Things to Say

I never look for things to say.
They find me and they crush my jaw.
They stop my mouth and mash my clay.
The slightest feather burns me raw.
They seek me where I cannot hide.
The air, the pollen and the leaf
Pursue me into omnicide
And pack my wordlessness in grief.

The Halfway Line

The scorpions in the bottle squirmed,
So mad with greed or zeal or hate,
That no one cared what thing he harmed:
Himself, his rival or his mate.

The bottle crashed, but each still stretched
His claws towards the halfway line
Marked on the broken glass, and retched
Out venom from an absent spine.

In Touch

If you can do so, read these words at night.
Lie down as if to sleep, turn off the light.

Now read me with your hands, as light as Braille.
My words may fail you, but your touch won't fail.

It will make true what now my heart can see –
You whom I don't know are in touch with me.

The cues of pain or grace are blind from birth,
Blind to the torque, blind to the tilt of earth.

Read out your words in lieu of mine, and I,
Far now, or dead, may ease them by and by.

Bright Darkness

My hands dissolve in water.
My body wastes away.
The air drifts past and through me
Each night and every day.

Bright darkness is my comfort,
Dark daylight is my friend,
And even I can't reckon
Where I subsist or end.

Not Now, Not Soon

Not now, not soon, but not too far,
May you not still be as you are,
Untouched by love for any being,
Unsearable, unstung, unseeing.
May you know love, and may it be
Returned to you as willingly.
If not, well, may you love in vain,
And know, if not that joy, this pain.

One Morning

One morning when the world was dark
My feet led me towards the park.
A blackbird sang an easy tune.
A contrail underlined the moon.
Dark horses crushed the plane leaves, white
With frost, then galloped out of sight,
And distant traffic, with a sound
Like muffled thunder, sped around.

Rose light enflamed the eastern sky.
A greyhound, masterless, loped by.
A poplar's black denuded crest
Thinned to reveal a magpie's nest.
On the red lake two snowy geese
Swam in a sarabande of peace,
And as I breathed the callous air
I lost the drift of my despair.

Parrots at Sunset

The parrots pair and nest
Now day is almost done.
Earth rises in the west
Against the reddened sun.

The hills assert their ranks –
Near, far and farther yet.
I give uncertain thanks
For the one world I'll get.

One sun, not two; one moon,
Not three. Four decades more,
I'd say, at most – and soon
I too, like those before

Who saw some rose-ringed pair
Of parrots court and nest,
Will, mixed with fire and air,
Disperse myself to rest.

The Yellow Leaves

The yellow leaves glint by; the branches merge and part;
    The clouds move past the window brightly.
What is this heaviness that won't unclench my heart,
    My work by day, my spirit nightly?

The year has months to go, the house is much the same,
    The universe is undiminished;
Nor is the darkness new, nor this ungiving game
    That waits till it or I am finished.

Day and Night

This was a day that came and went.
I don't know how the day was spent.
The sun rose up and reached its height.
The sun went down and it was night.
Somehow the hours that passed between
Dispersed as if they'd never been
Though I attended every one
Till both the day and I were done.

Sleepless, exhausted and perplexed,
Not knowing what is coming next,
I sense the stab of causeless fears,
The tedium of pointless tears.
Lonely, yet lacking will to find
One who could ease my limbs and mind,
I wait once more for faceless day
To blind the peaceless night away.

Late at Night

Late at night I lay awake,
Hearing in my spirit's ache
Voices I had eased away
In the bright forgiving day.

Through the hours of truth I heard
Like the driven fever-bird
Flinging out its cries of three
Every voice accusing me

Till I cried out in my fear:
Here I am, and you are here.
You can halt my heart, I know.
Do it then and let me go.

But the voices, soft somehow,
Whispered to my spirit now:
Live you must, for we must too
And we have no home but you.

Prayer for my Novel

Whatever force outside me moves my hand
And gives me strength to dream and understand,
Let me, by grace enlivened and by skill,
Enliven those who lived, and those who will.

The Shapes of Things

The shapes of things that are not here
Appear, disperse, and reappear:
A room, a face, a photograph,
A book, a letter or a laugh,
A turn of phrase or hand or mind,
Ungiven gifts you've left behind,
Each day recall themselves to me,
Altered into reality.

Things that are here and were before,
These too are altered at the core:
This pen, this bunch of keys, this chair,
The towel you used to dry your hair,
The song you sang whose words I knew
A year before I'd heard of you,
Even these hands, that felt your touch,
Though much the same, have altered much.

Red Rock

for Roger Howe

At Red Rock beach the waves come in.
The oystercatchers flap away.
The sun sinks into sand and skin
At four o'clock on Boxing Day.
    The bass thump of a volleyball
    Resounds below a skua's call.

The toddlers flap like little seals
Towards the magnet of the ocean,
Ignoring piteous appeals
From mothers bright with suntan lotion.
    I drink a bitter and a stout,
    Swim for a bit, and come back out.

The curved creek-current thrusts us through
Towards the sea, then back to shore.
To close the ring of gold and blue
We walk across the sand once more
    And float along the current's length,
    Resisting nothing but our strength.

And there – beyond the surf – a fin!
A curved back – and another – three!
Three dolphins ballet in the din
In bottle-nosed felicity.

How beautiful! They turn to greet us.
We love them, since they cannot eat us.

Ah, may it always be like this –
But '92's another year,
And an unkind antithesis
Lurks in a colder hemisphere.
    Advance, advance, Australia Fair –
    Next year I'll freeze, though God knows where.

In Shimla, fingernumbed and scowling,
In New York on a chilblained street,
In London with the north wind howling
Or vile Vienna in the sleet.
    Yet I'll be warm wherever I go
    If Red Rock burns beneath the snow.

Evening Scene from my Table

Evening is here, and I am here
At my baize table with a glass,
Now sipping my unfizzy beer,
Now looking out where on the grass

Two striped and crested hoopoes glean
Delicious insects one by one.
A barbet flies into the scene
Across the smoky city sun.

My friends have left, and I can see
No one, and no one will appear.
This must be happiness, to be
Sitting alone with birds and beer.

In a brief while the sun will go,
And grand unnerving bats will fly
Westward in clumped formations, slow
And dark across a darkened sky.

Haiku

through the winter night
sleep won't come and thoughts go round:
yowling cats on heat

finally at dawn
through my lids a sense of light,
in my mind a dream

i have lost the key,
now i'm flying, now i'm late,
now the dream lets go

safe in my razai
from the cold, i wonder how
i can hear this buzz

a mosquito's here –
out of season, out of tune,
homing in on blood

let me sleep in peace,
o mosquito, fact or dream,
till the crack of noon

~

then i'll get to work:
seven novels, seven plays,
seven children's tales

through the trees they sing
– sagging cables, unmaintained –
songs of speech and light

doors, bicycle bells,
sounds of cricket, car horns, dogs,
hawkers' cries and crows

sunset through the smoke
of the city to the west;
to the east a moon

full and gold and still;
by the wall the neighbour's guard
crouches by his fire

i too once was young
and these eyes that watch these hands
were not as they are

sometimes i recall
something of another face,
of another touch

just one room is left.
what may i put in it now
that there's not much time?

Tripping on a Bus

This is the schedule –
Give it away!
(Let it not stay.)
Give it to the lady –
The lady?
The lady who draws so beautifully
A face from Holbein,
Seated in the Greyhound bus depot
Waiting to go
To San Diego.
Give something to the lady.
(A smile, a cookie, a message . . .)

I see no lady.
An old woman, tired of despair,
Dreaming that tonight she will be happy
And put away sorrow for a year or two.
There will be sunflowers,
The scent of juniper, hay.
There will be coffee, the love of grandchildren.
Birthdays will be remembered . . .
She looks at the lovers with interest.

The sour conductor opens the gate.
Everyone is happy –
But look, the lovers are not happy –

They embrace, she is embracing him and crying.
He is saying something, she is not replying.
I think he is saying, 'Come back soon.'
(But she is not going to the moon.)
The lady looks perplexed and does not know
If this is the bus to San Diego.
The sour conductor's cheeks begin to glow –
'See, lady, see this sign – it says San Diego. S, A, N . . .'
The lady looks dignified. The lovers embrace again.

Not a word, not a word through the journey.
We look out the window:
A nuclear plant – two scoops of radioactive ice-cream –
Disneyland – where life is but a dream –
The crisp line of the sea . . .
I look at the lady.
O God! She too is crying,
As if a world were dying.
The sunset burns out with a terrible glow.
The bus pours on towards San Diego.

Tercets to Parsnip

Do not go screaming into that good pot.
Some like it tepid and some like it hot.
Some like your crossword and some like it not.

I've finished it. Would that I'd not begun.
Fine words were there, but when all's said and done,
They margarined a parsnip, buttered none.

The Infinite

This lonely hill was always dear to me
And this hedge too, that keeps so large a part
Of the ultimate horizon from my view.
But as I sit and gaze, interminable
Spaces beyond it come to mind, unearthly
Silences, and deep, deep quiet – and for
A little while my heart lets go its fear.
And as I listen to the wind storm through
These branches, I compare its voice to that
Infinite silence; and eternity
Comes to my mind, all the dead ages, all
That lives and is, and all its noise. In this
Immensity my thoughts drown, and it is
Sweet to me to be shipwrecked in this sea.

Giacomo Leopardi

To the Moon

O gracious moon, I recall how last year
I came to this hill and watched you, full of pain,
And you hung there over that wood, just as
You do now and fill everything with light.
But nebulous and tremulous through the tears
That filled my eyes, your face appeared to me,
So troubled was my life; and is; nor has
It changed its style, beloved moon. And yet
It gives me pleasure to remember and
To count the stages of my sorrow. How
Pleasant it is, when one is young, and the path
Of hope is long and that of memory short,
To call to mind once more things from the past,
However sad, and though the pain endures.

Giacomo Leopardi

Sonnet

I can't love anyone who isn't you.
I don't know how to. No, my lady, no –
Venus herself could come to earth below
And not delight my heart the way you do.

So sweet, so gracious are these eyes I view,
A single glance from them is like a blow
That kills me, while the next one may bestow
Life where the first gave death – two worlds in two!

If I lived for five hundred thousand years,
Believe me, dearest love, and trust your ears:
I could love no one else – no one, nowhere.

I'd have to fashion other veins; my own
Are now so filled with love for you alone,
Nobody else could find a lodging there.

Pierre de Ronsard

In a Small Garden in Venice

You and the girls will come back in a week
From your long Russian summer sojourn – and I,
Who haven't used it, will relinquish it.
Today I came to see if the plants were parched,
Sat at this wooden table, and claimed its peace.
I reach up to the trellis and taste a grape.
Which shall I crush with these too-restless fingers:
Rosemary, lavender – or that tomato leaf
Within whose shadow a gecko climbs the wall?
Domestic sounds are all I hear – a bottle,
Footsteps, a muted radio; the canal,
Its engine-gusts and thrum, is far away.
Few folk walk down the calle. This nest is green.
The sky is cobalt. Dull geraniums
Mark, but don't blare forth from the house beyond
That wall of yellow stucco and of stone.
The shutters are all shut and I'm alone.

   Alone? Not quite. For in the small dark room
Just within doors with a table and narrow bed
– Cool, cool, a sanctum from this blaze of blue –
Two oval portraits, prints in black and white,
Lean on a shelf; one of them, Pushkin, who
Never stepped out of Russia in his life,
Let alone roamed around this town, but who
Belongs to you who know his works by heart

And, yes, to me, who, though I cannot read
A word of his by eye, know him by soul.
I wouldn't be here, were it not for him.
He gave me me. This morning, when I turned
The rabbit-key lent by your younger daughter,
I thought of visiting him, yet feared I'd lose
All that I had marked out to do today
By standing in a trance, held by his eyes,
His replicated, ageless paper eyes,
As once I stood five hours holding his book
In Stanford Bookstore, and forgot all else
– My economics lectures, food and drink,
Appointments, unpaid bills, the world, my friends,
Myself – what? – almost thirty years ago.
Translation though it was, though every Russian
– Yes, you included, when I met you first,
Before the concert in that cavernous room –
Shakes her head slowly when I mention this
In wistful sympathy ('What can they get
From Pushkin who can't understand our tongue?'),
Yet what I got, I got – and it got me
Out of myself, into myself, and made me
Set everything aside I'd set my thoughts on,
And grasp my time, live in his rooms and write
What even today puzzles me by its birth,
The Golden Gate, that sad and happy thing,
Child of my youth, my first wild fictive fling.

   The sun has edged itself across the table
Under the trellis. Now my mobile phone
Has turned too hot to touch, and now my head

Has turned too hot to think with, and I've come
Withindoors and am lying on the bed,
Limbs loose, hands slack. Pushkin looks down on me
As sleep and desperation melt my brain.
A clock ticks softly; on its face, IV
Instead of four I's, marks the hour of four.
My eyes begin to close, the sea to roar.

Howling with fear, an Adriatic storm
Washes across the Black and Baltic Seas.
The Tiber teems with sharks; St Petersburg
Froths white with eels and monkfish, while a pike
Twelve metres long patrols the Grand Canal,
Capsizing gondolas and eating all
The honeymooning couples it can find.
I ply my small shikara filled with flowers
From shore to houseboat and to shore again,
Singing to ease the seas and the sad hearts
Of those who have lost friends to tooth and fin,
To eely turbulence and monkfish roil,
Casting chrysanthemums upon the waves
To calm the agony of single souls,
All those whose lovers are with them no more,
Till all is still on houseboat and on shore.

And then I find myself alive once more
(Although I would have been content to end
Somewhere within that world) and since I am,
I wander out into the humid, green
And shadowless – now clouds obscure the sun –
Small garden where a gecko climbs a wall.

The lilies of the valley in the well,
That roundel filled with mud, are flowerless.
Mosquitoes range at will, squat pigeons flap
Around me in the heavy air, the grapes
Look plump and green and sinister – and the steps
I hear beyond the wall, more frequent now
That it's the hour to go back home, speak out
Like a soft tattoo on an untuned drum:
Return to where you're loved, to the sound of a spoon
Against the wall of a pan, to a welcoming voice –
And I imagine someone pouring out
A glass of something under the trellised growth
To me and my companions, poets both.
Crushed grape within fused sand; they smile at me,
Nod at each other and drink silently.
The gecko does not speak and nor do they.
They have said all they came to earth to say.
Alone again, I toy with what they've left:
Fashioned from the lagoon, a common gift.
I turn the hourglass to re-sieve its sands,
A fragile monument half-built by hands.

Minterne: Four Poems

commissioned by Veronica Stewart for the Lady Digby to celebrate the 45th anniversary of the Summer Music Society of Dorset, set to music by Jonathan Dove and performed on 30 August 2007 in Minterne, Dorset by Patricia Rozario (soprano), Philippe Honoré (violin) and Steven Isserlis (cello)

1768; 2007

The roar
Of cannon shot
From shattered men-of-war,
The smoke, the screams of pain, the hot
Shudder of battle past, he turns to greet
The arts of peace for war, and for salt-water sweet:
Cascade and lake and stream and pool, not one straight line
– Even an oval cellar for his wine –
His sails furled up, his oaks and turf
Set down and, far from shore,
Of wind, not surf,
The roar.

Clear chords
And melody,
Still more than sails and swords
– Though born a daughter of the sea –
Give her delight – or both delight and pain,
Since music lives in each, and quickens each again.
Close on these walls rest snake and dove: an ancient tune
Entwining grief with joy, and night with noon.
All this she hears – and shares with love,
With words or without words,
Rich decades of
Clear chords.

Which Way?

Should I then say, can I then know
   Which way the wind should blow –
Across the grass, beyond the mulberry tree?
     For now I see
The sky in tatters – all the clouds awry
   And soon I will not see the sky.
   It will be closed, I will be dead
And all I wish to say will stay unsaid.

How could I know, when first I came,
   Nothing would be the same?
Where is the hedge, where is the hill beyond?
     No reed or frond,
No lake – a zone of mist, in which I stray,
   And soon I will have lost my way.
   Alone, I wander where I choose,
And soon there will not be a me to lose.

Rocking-Horse

Now there's something something Waterloo and
    something Tráfalgár
And it's far too sunny nowadays, too sunny, yes, by far –
And all I really want to do is ride a camel through
The Kalahari desert and across the Great Karoo.

Oh the confidence of houses with a rocking-horse or three,
Oh the ducks and coots that swim across a blue infinity,
Oh the dry-rot and the wet-rot and the loneliness of beams
And the empty Bath and Garter and the solid stuff of
    dreams.

Now the afternoon is burning and it must be half past
    three
And Mama is getting restless, but that doesn't bother me
And Papa is fighting France today unless he's fighting
    Spain
And I'm either three or thirty – which I'll never be again

And the day is past and passing and the afternoon is hot
And it's something something Waterloo unless, of course,
    it's not –
And it's tugging of the forelock or the foreskin to the
    squire
And the people down from London and the gentry of the
    shire   ~

And the music music music and the trees and trees and
    trees
And the duty to one's neighbours and the conquest of the
    seas
And this little nook of England and this heritage so rare
And the universe goes onwards and it doesn't really care

But it's ninety-six for seven and it's seventeen to three
And it's nine to four against us and it's getting late for tea
But the fig-tree has the oak-tree in an afternoon of fears
And the rocking-horse is sinking and the jockey is in tears

And the afternoon is fading and the tapestry is torn
And the universe is dying and the Aubusson is worn
But I love to sing regardless and I'll sing until I drop
But now the song is over and I don't know how to stop

So I'm something something singing in a something
    something song
And you're very very welcome to keep mum or sing along
But my baby brother's crying and the mercury is high
So until tomorrow afternoon I have to say goodbye.

The Tree of Many Names

One morning, one morning in May
As we strolled hand in hand beneath the tree
The sun rose. We could see
The fluttering doves emerge from out the mist.
There was no more to say.
We kissed.

One evening, one evening in May
As I strolled by myself beneath the tree
The moon rose. I could see
The handkerchiefs that shivered as they slept.
There was no more to say.
I wept.

One midnight, one midnight in May
As, old at last, I strolled beneath the tree
The starlight let me see
The trembling ghosts that wooed me as they cried.
There was no more to say.
I died.

***

Suzhou Canal on a June Night

I close my eyes to sense.
Above, a magpie cries.
Magnolias shed their scent.
The North wind soughs and sighs.

It brings the petals down
To graze against my hand.
The dialect of the town
Comes to me where I stand:

Softvoiced and liquid speech
Of quietcultured folk,
Two women's voices, each
Mellifluous. I stroke

The parapet of the bridge,
Held by the blind delight,
The sense of privilege
Of being here tonight.

The turning wind asserts
The foetid, useful noise
Of the canal. Late boats
Unload. With opened eyes

~

I see the boats swing through
Below me, and my gaze
Turns to the distant roofs,
To unrecovered days,

While in curved dark above
A half-obscured half-moon
Now jokes of endless love,
Now mourns for passing June.

The Forms Lie on the Table

The forms lie on the table, the paperclip removed.
The animal-cycle table is unfolded.
'What's your name?' I ask the staring boy.
The boy carefully spits on the floor, and smiles.

His grandfather puffs at his Double Happiness cigarette
And thinks of cement and lintels; he and his son
Are building a house, and forms are outside his ken
But he is polite and describes his expenditures.

The accountant's door faces panels of green
As yet untransplanted rice. Three women pass,
Bearing the harvested rape. The old man sighs
And says, 'My second brother was a pig.'

'That makes him 45 years old'; I fill the space
With a Bic pen. The boy looks at it
With wonderment at its transparency.
A picture of Lady White Snake looks down from the wall.

The abacus clicks, a chicken strays into the room.
The old man says that the Japanese burnt and killed.
The accountant mentions the Guomindang conscriptions.
The boy has heard this before and strokes his chin.   ~

A weasel runs along the embankment of the fields
And into the standing stalks. The golden goslings
Struggle into the pond. The oxen bolt
Towards the wheat despite the woman's curses.

And there beyond the trees the Great River flows
And flows onwards and onwards and its rippled gold
Pours itself onwards past the mulberry hills
And the investigators and investigated and the black tiles
    of roofs.

Dark

Now night.
The buses hum.
Cicadas –
It will not come,

The mood of night,
Of letting be,
Of letting darkness
Enter me.

The fear that oozed
Through sun and dust
Is moon-appeased.
I must

Not tremble for what died
Nor mourn for culm or grain
But case the root
For spring to quicken again.

For spring, for dawn
Against the stun of light.
Let it be. Let it grow.
Let there not be light.

A Winter Room

The sparrows bob from frosty twig to twig
Against an under-lit sky.
She sets down her cup and laughs.
When he asks why,
She says they remind her of something.
It would be too tedious to explain.
Nothing, no, she's not being secretive.
She laughs again.

How could he not be happy
Sitting here in this chair,
Hearing her laughter thaw the room,
He here, she there?
She gets up, goes to the sill.
He stirs his tea,
Sips, frowns, joins her at the window.
They watch the frozen tree.

Western Highlands

Across the loch, its surface malachite-pure,
The mist unravels from the farther shore.
I stumble upon a track in the faltering light.
Grey-veiled red deer pause in the stance of flight.

Full Circle

The circle from indifference
To new indifference
For you is perfect, but for me
The present still is tense
With rigid reminiscences that come
Unwished – of you, your home.

Gently I sift this great compacted
Stock of memories:
The house whose name evokes the wind
Through early-woken trees
Growing around and sheltering the lawn
With silhouettes of dawn;

How fine you looked, after hard mowing,
Resting in the clear shade;
And when, with the first touch of evening,
With casual skill you made
The hearth's full complement of log and coal
Blaze with a wild control;

The room of the two keyboards where,
Unwinding, we fed ourselves
On Bach; the files of bright-spined books
Ranged on its heavy shelves

Through which on spendthrift afternoons we browsed;
The warm and open house.

Last night when from that pitted roadway
I wandered as I dreamt,
The trees were bent, hostile, entangled,
Weeds massed and grass unkempt,
The house locked and the only key inside;
Ingress denied.

No Further War

We are the last generations; Surdas, Bach,
Rembrandt, Du Fu, all life, love, work and worth
Will end in the particular rain; no ark
Will screen its force, no prayer procure rebirth.
The government of nations is assigned
Sage, journeyman and lunatic by rota;
A couple of toxic madmen sting mankind
Each century; we won't escape the quota.
Dead planet of an unimportant star,
Beautiful earth, whose radiant creation
Became too radiant, no further war,
No suffering, frenzy or recrimination
Will litter your denatured crust or mar
Your deepening entropy with agitation.

Spring Morning

Wistaria tremble in the breeze.
As he hangs out his sheets, he hears
The medley of a mockingbird
Leap from a live-oak into his yard.
Two sparrows quarrel as they pass
To ruffle the sunned and shadowed grass,
Emerald with March rain, rich with weeds.
He thinks a little of his needs.

Sunday. He wraps a sourdough loaf
In foil and puts it in the stove.
No cat. No paper. No telephone.
His balance: that he is alone.
Light; work; a postcard from a friend.
He sees, as he breakfasts in a band
Of sun, pollen float through the door
Onto the breadcrumbs on the floor.

Meanwhile, cerulean days extend
Perturblessly without an end.
Wistaria or a sparrows' feud
Or ants adventuring through a wood
Of tall grass, let his heart be free
Of grand ferment. If eternity
Is long, he can link days to days.
The sun is generous; there are ways.

Cloud-Cancers

White on the sheet of night they fly,
Gulls, gliding on the ferry's smoke,
 While the waves lunge and lapse
 Along the delusive kelp-strung shore.

Here too the motion of the earth
Is palpable; here too he gives
 Himself to the place, the being,
 Changeable, that will not betray.

Cloud-cancers grip the derelict Bear.
There is no bitterness in his thoughts.
 He cannot believe, but prays
 To night, the earth, the moon, the waves,

This permanent and inconstant sea.
The great seals stare, while from the dark
 Gulls' yawp or sharp unsifted
 Echo of song exhausts his ears.

Old in his soul? The tapering mist,
Like unedged knowledge of love, sustains
 His heart till a new light,
 Slow to dawn, dawns in its time.

Index of First and Last Lines

My hands dissolve in water   20

Nobody else could find a lodging there   39
Not now, not soon, but not too far   21
Now mourns for passing June   51
Now night   54
Now there's something something Waterloo and
    something Tráfalgár   47

O gracious moon, I recall how last year   38
One morning, one morning in May   49
One morning when the world was dark   22
Out venom from an absent spine   18

Should I then say, can I then know   46
Since there is nothing left but this   1
Slow to dawn, dawns in its time   61
So until tomorrow afternoon I have to say goodbye   48
Sweet to me to be shipwrecked in this sea   37

that there's not much time?   33
That waits till it or I am finished   24
The bus pours on towards San Diego   35
The circle from indifference   57
The forms lie on the table, the paperclip removed   52
The parrots pair and nest   23
The roar   45
The scorpions in the bottle squirmed   18
The shapes of things that are not here   28
The sparrows bob from frosty twig to twig   55
The sun is generous; there are ways   60

The yellow leaves glint by; the branches merge and
   part   24
They margarined a parsnip, buttered none   36
They watch the frozen tree   55
This is the schedule   34
This lonely hill was always dear to me   37
This was a day that came and went   25
Though much the same, have altered much   28
through the winter night   32
To blind the peaceless night away   25

We are the last generations; Surdas, Bach   59
Whatever force outside me moves my hand   27
Where I subsist or end   20
White on the sheet of night they fly   61
Wistaria tremble in the breeze   60

You and the girls will come back in a week   40
Your deepening entropy with agitation   59